TEN BASIC LESSONS IN

PRAYER

CHARLES MWEWA

DEDICATION

For

Those who want to know more
about God and the God of prayer.

CONTENTS

INTRODUCTION

This little book of a lesson in prayer is based on the Prayer of Solomon when he was dedicating the temple, the project his father David had bequeathed to him.

Then spake Solomon, The LORD said that he would dwell in the thick darkness.
13 I have surely built thee an house to dwell in, a settled place for thee to abide in for ever.
14 And the king turned his face about, and blessed all the congregation of Israel: (and all the congregation of Israel stood;)
15 And he said, Blessed be the LORD God of Israel, which spake with his mouth unto David my father, and hath with his hand fulfilled it, saying,
16 Since the day that I brought forth my people Israel out of Egypt, I chose no city out of all the tribes of Israel to build an house, that my name might be therein; but I chose David to be over my people Israel.
17 And it was in the heart of David my father to build an house for the name of the LORD God of Israel.
18 And the LORD said unto David my father, Whereas it was in thine heart to build an house unto my name, thou didst well that it was in thine heart.
19 Nevertheless thou shalt not build the house; but thy son that shall come forth out of thy loins, he shall build the house unto my name.

20 And the LORD hath performed his word that he spake, and I am risen up in the room of David my father, and sit on the throne of Israel, as the LORD promised, and have built an house for the name of the LORD God of Israel.

21 And I have set there a place for the ark, wherein is the covenant of the LORD, which he made with our fathers, when he brought them out of the land of Egypt.

22 And Solomon stood before the altar of the LORD in the presence of all the congregation of Israel, and spread forth his hands toward heaven:

23 And he said, LORD God of Israel, there is no God like thee, in heaven above, or on earth beneath, who keepest covenant and mercy with thy servants that walk before thee with all their heart:

24 Who hast kept with thy servant David my father that thou promisedst him: thou spakest also with thy mouth, and hast fulfilled it with thine hand, as it is this day.

25 Therefore now, LORD God of Israel, keep with thy servant David my father that thou promisedst him, saying, There shall not fail thee a man in my sight to sit on the throne of Israel; so that thy children take heed to their way, that they walk before me as thou hast walked before me.

26 And now, O God of Israel, let thy word, I pray thee, be verified, which thou spakest unto thy servant David my father.

27 But will God indeed dwell on the earth? behold, the heaven and heaven of heavens

cannot contain thee; how much less this house that I have builded?

28 Yet have thou respect unto the prayer of thy servant, and to his supplication, O LORD my God, to hearken unto the cry and to the prayer, which thy servant prayeth before thee to day:

29 That thine eyes may be open toward this house night and day, even toward the place of which thou hast said, My name shall be there: that thou mayest hearken unto the prayer which thy servant shall make toward this place.

30 And hearken thou to the supplication of thy servant, and of thy people Israel, when they shall pray toward this place: and hear thou in heaven thy dwelling place: and when thou hearest, forgive.

31 If any man trespass against his neighbour, and an oath be laid upon him to cause him to swear, and the oath come before thine altar in this house:

32 Then hear thou in heaven, and do, and judge thy servants, condemning the wicked, to bring his way upon his head; and justifying the righteous, to give him according to his righteousness.

33 When thy people Israel be smitten down before the enemy, because they have sinned against thee, and shall turn again to thee, and confess thy name, and pray, and make supplication unto thee in this house:

34 Then hear thou in heaven, and forgive the sin of thy people Israel, and bring them again unto the land which thou gavest unto their fathers.

35 When heaven is shut up, and there is no rain, because they have sinned against thee; if they pray toward this place, and confess thy name, and turn from their sin, when thou afflictest them:

36 Then hear thou in heaven, and forgive the sin of thy servants, and of thy people Israel, that thou teach them the good way wherein they should walk, and give rain upon thy land, which thou hast given to thy people for an inheritance.

37 If there be in the land famine, if there be pestilence, blasting, mildew, locust, or if there be caterpiller; if their enemy besiege them in the land of their cities; whatsoever plague, whatsoever sickness there be;

38 What prayer and supplication soever be made by any man, or by all thy people Israel, which shall know every man the plague of his own heart, and spread forth his hands toward this house:

39 Then hear thou in heaven thy dwelling place, and forgive, and do, and give to every man according to his ways, whose heart thou knowest; (for thou, even thou only, knowest the hearts of all the children of men;)

40 That they may fear thee all the days that they live in the land which thou gavest unto our fathers.

41 Moreover concerning a stranger, that is not of thy people Israel, but cometh out of a far country for thy name's sake;

42 (For they shall hear of thy great name, and of thy strong hand, and of thy stretched out arm;) when he shall come and pray toward this house;

43 Hear thou in heaven thy dwelling place, and do according to all that the stranger calleth to thee for: that all people of the earth may know thy name, to fear thee, as do thy people Israel; and that they may know that this house, which I have builded, is called by thy name.

44 If thy people go out to battle against their enemy, whithersoever thou shalt send them, and shall pray unto the LORD toward the city which thou hast chosen, and toward the house that I have built for thy name:

45 Then hear thou in heaven their prayer and their supplication, and maintain their cause.

46 If they sin against thee, (for there is no man that sinneth not,) and thou be angry with them, and deliver them to the enemy, so that they carry them away captives unto the land of the enemy, far or near;

47 Yet if they shall bethink themselves in the land whither they were carried captives, and repent, and make supplication unto thee in the land of them that carried them captives, saying, We have sinned, and have done perversely, we have committed wickedness;

48 And so return unto thee with all their heart, and with all their soul, in the land of their enemies, which led them away captive, and pray unto thee toward their land, which thou gavest unto their fathers, the city which thou hast chosen, and the house which I have built for thy name:

49 Then hear thou their prayer and their supplication in heaven thy dwelling place, and maintain their cause,

50 And forgive thy people that have sinned against thee, and all their transgressions

wherein they have transgressed against thee, and give them compassion before them who carried them captive, that they may have compassion on them:

51 For they be thy people, and thine inheritance, which thou broughtest forth out of Egypt, from the midst of the furnace of iron:

52 That thine eyes may be open unto the supplication of thy servant, and unto the supplication of thy people Israel, to hearken unto them in all that they call for unto thee.

53 For thou didst separate them from among all the people of the earth, to be thine inheritance, as thou spakest by the hand of Moses thy servant, when thou broughtest our fathers out of Egypt, O LORD God.

54 And it was so, that when Solomon had made an end of praying all this prayer and supplication unto the LORD, he arose from before the altar of the LORD, from kneeling on his knees with his hands spread up to heaven.

55 And he stood, and blessed all the congregation of Israel with a loud voice, saying,

56 Blessed be the LORD, that hath given rest unto his people Israel, according to all that he promised: there hath not failed one word of all his good promise, which he promised by the hand of Moses his servant.

57 The LORD our God be with us, as he was with our fathers: let him not leave us, nor forsake us:

58 That he may incline our hearts unto him, to walk in all his ways, and to keep his

commandments, and his statutes, and his
judgments, which he commanded our fathers.
[59] And let these my words, wherewith I have
made supplication before the LORD, be nigh
unto the LORD our God day and night, that he
maintain the cause of his servant, and the
cause of his people Israel at all times, as the
matter shall require:
[60] That all the people of the earth may know
that the LORD is God, and that there is none
else.
[61] Let your heart therefore be perfect with
the LORD our God, to walk in his statutes, and
to keep his commandments, as at this day.
[62] And the king, and all Israel with him,
offered sacrifice before the LORD.[1]

From this prayer, we learn about ten (10) basic lessons
in prayer. Each chapter ends with an anecdotal
summary of the main point.

c.m.

---

[1] 1 Kings 8:12-62 (King James version – KJV)

1 | REVELATION

Revelation is an act of prayer. It is an indication to pray. It is a sensation, a prompting, a desire God places on our minds and hearts to pray.

What God has revealed will only become effective when we take it back to God in prayer. This revelation, a prompting, is an act of faith manifesting through our emotions and feelings.

Many times, when you feel like praying or praying for someone or something, it is not just a hunch, it could be God the Holy Spirit moving you to action.

In the Bible we read, "For you, O LORD of hosts, God of Israel, have revealed this to your servant…"[2]

Chapter Summary

> *Revelation, and not judgment or need, should be the main motivation to pray. God's promises are based on the revealed Word of God.*

---

[2] 2 Samuel 7:27

2 | AUDIENCE

Audience with God in prayer should be sought after as an act of deliberate desire. Our great dignitaries such as kings, presidents, etc., are a busy lot. But even by virtue of their positions, they demand protocol and a high level of procedure.

To see them we go to certain lengths and extremes. Seeing them we must and so we make appointments and frantic efforts until we finally have an audience with them.

While in prayer the way has been paved for us through the blood of Jesus, we still, like ancient people, need to ask God to hear us.

We go even further; we must ask God to actually answer our prayers. Prayer is our active adoration, supplication, or intercession, beseeching the throne of God that he should choose to answer us and not do anything else.

In John we read, "And whatever you ask in my name, that I will do, that the Father may be glorified in the Son. If you ask anything in my name, I will do it."[3] The Father responds to us through the Son. The Son allows us to petition His Father for Him to answer us. Prayer is, therefore, inevitable to having an audience with God.

In the Bible we read, "O LORD, my God, listen to the cry and the prayer which your servant is praying before you today."[4]

Chapter Summary

> *"Let us therefore come boldly unto the throne of grace, that we may obtain mercy, and find grace to help in time of need" – Hebrews 4:16*

---

[3] John 14:13-17
[4] 1 Kings 8:28

3 | PROMISES

Promises ought to be evoked in prayer. Take to God back what He has said He would do. Remind God of His promises towards you, others, or the nation.

What God has said He would perform will not be performed unless we ask Him to fulfill it through prayer.

Solomon reminded God of His promises: "That your eyes may be open towards this temple night and day, towards the place of which you said, 'My name shall be there.'"[5]

The human race is God's experiment. There is no similarly situated creature He has

---

[5] 1 Kings 8:29

endowed with such graces and blessings as the will, as the humans. With our will God cannot dictate terms against our will. Our relationship, therefore, is based on what each one promises the other.

Just as God holds us accountable to our words, we also do to His Word. It is one of the grandest reasons why He went to lengths to have His promises recorded and documented in scripts, the quintessential one being the Bible.

He is a God of covenant. Read and pray back His promises for you to Him. He will honor them all.

Chapter Summary

> *God is haste to do what He has promised. Good news is that God has promised us everything, but it is only prayer that is key to unlocking the richness of His promises.*

4 | "PLAGUE OF THE HEART"

The "plague of the heart," is the deepest fear, anxiety, sin, or habit that you know is not pleasing unto God.

Everyone should know what that plague is and spread it bare before God in prayer. It is the first roadblock to answered prayer. It is the first hindrance to our own prayers. It must be eliminated first before God can begin to consider our prayers.

It is a wall that stands between us and God. When it is gone, we can now ask God or demand for anything we want or seek from God in prayer.

In the Bible we read, "Whatever prayer, whatever supplication is made by anyone, or by all your people Israel, when each one knows the plague of his own heart…"[6]

In reality, this plague is removed when we first pray the "Sinner's Prayer," whether consciously through an altar call or unconsciously through liturgy or church invocation and ritual.

It is the first time we acknowledged the need for God and articulated our belief through our mouth or another form of confession.

Once that way is opened, we constantly are reminded of our own frailties and the need to confess sins through the Holy Spirit's-initiated process of sanctification.

God forgives every sin that has been confessed: "If we confess our sins, He is faithful and just to forgive us our sins and to cleanse us from all unrighteousness."[7]

Chapter Summary

> *"Now we know that God does not hear sinners,"* *(John 9:31), but He hears a sinner's prayer.*

---

[6] 1 Kings 8:38
[7] 1 John 1:9

5 | CAUSE MAINTENANCE

The "maintain their cause"[8] idea illustrates our own desire and wants and wills.

Indeed, the will of God is to be desired and evoked in prayer. But that is in as far as we want to exist in time and occupy space. God first put His will in us as our deepest desire, a talent, a gift, or ability.

We are born a complete package. It is very easy to overrule our talents and abilities as worldly and miss the will of God. Sometimes, people erroneously think that doing God's will

---

[8] 1 Kings 8:45, 49

is only if we are preaching or teaching God's word.

That is an incomplete list.

The will of God is *this* thing in us which we so desire to see happen, which drives us to action, which gives us extraordinary impetus to work and achieve, which will translate into what God's will is for us here on earth.

God first created us to enjoy Him, not to preach or teach. That came with the Fall of Adam and Eve. In us is God's kingdom and we fulfill it with the abilities and enablement and natural gifts He has placed in us.

The New Testament records: "For it is God who works in you, both to will and to work for his good pleasure."[9]

Indeed, God is working. He is working in us. He provides every desire in us and the correspondent power or ability to do what He wills and pleases.

Do not dismiss the desire you have; it is God making His will for you known. Do it and fulfill your destiny.

God's will for us is not very much divorced from our own righteous or benevolent desires and goodwill. "Then hear in

---

[9] Philippians 2:13

heaven their prayer and their supplication and maintain their cause."[10]

Chapter Summary

> *"Behold, the kingdom of God is within you,"*
> *(Luke 17:21). We walk with God in us. Jesus*
> *Himself is Emmanuel — God is with us. Prayer is*
> *the declaration of our desires and wills to God.*

---

[10] 1 Kings 8:45, 49, *supra.*

6 | GOD'S EYES AND HEART

We must seek God's eyes and heart in prayer. Until God is able to see what we are praying for and to constantly look at our request with favor, and until His heart is in our prayer, we should not stop praying.

Prayer is seeking that God's eyes and heart will be with you always. It is grabbing God's attention; it is insisting that He looks at your request; it is persisting with your petition.

Prayer is letting God do nothing else but answer your supplication. When God's eyes are upon you and His heart is with you, you have God's presence with you. You will then be assured that every time you pray, He will see, and every time you think, He will be there to know. In the Bible we read: "I have heard your prayer…I have consecrated this house which you have built…My eyes and my heart will be there perpetually."[11]

Chapter Summary

> *"The eye is the lamp of the body. So, if your eye is healthy, your whole body will be full of light," (Matthew 6:22). And "You shall love the LORD your God with all of your heart, with all of your soul, and with all of your strength," (Mark 12:30-31). When God's eyes look at us, we receive grace and favor; when His heart is with us, we have eternal life. Prayer connects us to God's sight and to His heart.*

---

[11] 1 Kings 9:3

7 | LIFTED PRAYER

To "lift up your prayer" is an expression of our sincerity in prayer. We lift up our prayer when we desperately need God's intervention.

We lift up our prayer to God when we want Him to turn around in our favor. After we have done bad things or have been unfaithful to God or our fellow human beings, we come to God with lifted up prayer.

It is a cry; it is a deep expression of our deepest desire. When we have mistakenly spoken things, especially the things that we are not supposed to speak. Or if we have looked at things that we are not supposed to see. Or if we have gone to places where we are not supposed to go. Or if we have offended God, we ought to lift up our prayer in humbleness to God. In the Bible we read: "Therefore, lift up your prayer for the remnant that is left."[12]

Chapter Summary

> *A type of prayer called intercession is one where we lift up prayer for others. We must do so with fear and trembling since we, ourselves, are weak like our brothers and sisters whom we pray for. But for God's mercy and grace, we pray for others as for ourselves in the spirit and bond of love.*

---

[12] 2 Kings 19:4

8 | TEAR UP, IF POSSIBLE

Tears link us to our hearts. We can easily know the condition of our heart through our tears. When the heart is happy, it might produce tears. When the heart is sad, it might produce tears, too.

Our tears must be seen by God in prayer. Leaders must cry for their people in prayer, they must present the people's positions with emotions.

Tears expose the activities of the heart. The thing about tears is that in many cases (except, of course, in crocodile tearing) they do not misrepresent. We mostly cry in unusual emotional circumstances.

God knows that our tears speak of the genuineness of our petitions. Tears are a sign of a broken spirit, and that God will not despise.[13] In the Bible we read: "Thus says the LORD, the God of David your father: 'I have heard your prayer, I have seen your tears…'"[14]

Chapter Summary

> *Prayer, genuine prayer, involves both our spirits (faith) and souls (emotions). We ought to "feel" (with our bodies) God in our prayers though by faith we know that He is close to us, and He is a Spirit. Thus, prayer is an intricate, interwoven mingling of our entire being — body, soul and spirit.*

---

[13] See Psalm 51:17
[14] 2 Kings 20:5

9 | RESPECTIFULLY

God respects all our prayers. It is the only means He has revealed through which we can converse with Him. When we sit, stand, bow, or approach Him in prayer, He endears it. Prayer, by design, is an act of faith in the unseen God.

Respect for our prayers is God's number one commitment. Even before He knows our request or our purpose for praying, God will regard our prayers.

In essence, the act of approaching God itself means so much to God. When you decide that you will pray, for whatever reason, God is already committed to hearing you.

God respects or regards your intention to pray, and He places great admiration on your prayer. The Bible says: "Yet, regard the prayer of your servant…"[15]

Chapter Summary

Worship, praise, honor, respect, and duty are all core values in our walk with God. God is Sovereign; He deserves ultimate honor, regard, and respect. We ought to be intentional and give the highest homage to God: "Be still and know that I am God; I will be exalted among the nations, I will be exalted in the earth" (Psalm 46:10). But also, we ought not to fear to approach Him, because He is our Father and we are dearest to Him: "Behold, what manner of love the Father hath bestowed upon us, that we should be called the sons of God" (1 John 3). The balancing of these two graces, ensures success both in prayer and in our spiritual life.

---

[15] 2 Chronicles 6:19

10 | FINISH WELL, AMEN

Finish your prayer to God with an "Amen." This means that you agree or admit with God for the requests or adoration you have made. It means "let it be."

Prayer is a burden on our hearts. It heavily weighs on us until we off-load it unto the feet of Jesus.

When you are praying, do not rush to conclude your prayer, if and when it is necessary. A well-prayed prayer will bring you to a place where you are empty of the emotion, feeling or of the said desire. At that point, you will know your prayer is ended, and you can faithfully acclaim, "amen or it is done."

This should be as an act of faith, of consent, of admission with your inner self that what you have said or presented to God has all come off and you have nothing left.

It is also a strong testament with your heart that you have said all that is required of you in that moment.

It is further a *meeting of minds*, yours, and the Holy God's, that He has now absorbed you of your prayer and you can now walk away knowing that your matter has been settled.

"Amen or let it be" should not only be a religious ritual, a simplification of our impatience or a quick quote that pacifies our lack of time or sense of urgency.

It must be a testimony of our own internal agreement that we have given all, believed all, and expecting all from God. In the Bible we read: "And so it was when Solomon had finished praying all this prayer and supplication to the LORD, that *he arose from before* the altar of the LORD, from kneeling on his knees with his hands spread out to heaven."[16]

---

[16] 1 Kings 8:54, emphasis added.

Chapter Summary

> *"Whatever you bind on earth will be bound in heaven, and whatever you loose on earth will be loosed in heaven" (Matthew 18:18). This legal statement is a declaration of authority and finality in the matters of prayers of agreement and church discipline. However, for individuals, it is a statement of principle. When people on earth decide in the name of Jesus Christ, their decision is endorsed by heaven. When they pray, it is as good as done. "Amen" is a sign of confidence in the power of God who answers prayer. It is an assertion of faith and finality.*

ABOUT THE AUTHOR

Best Selling Author, Charles Mwewa (LLB; BA Law; BA Ed; LLM), is a prolific researcher, poet, novelist, lawyer, law professor and Christian apologist and intercessor. Mwewa has written no less than 78 books and counting in every genre and has exhibited his works at prestigious expos like the Ottawa International Book Expo and is the winner of the Coppa Awards for his signature publication, *Zambia: Struggles of My People.*

SELECTED BOOKS BY THIS AUTHOR

1. *ZAMBIA: Struggles of My People (First and Second Editions)*
2. *10 FINANCIAL & WEALTH ATTITUDES TO AVOID*
3. *10 STRATEGIES TO DEFEAT STRESS AND DEPRESSION: Creating an Internal Safeguard against Stress and Depression*
4. *100+ REASONS TO READ BOOKS*
5. *A CASE FOR AFRICA?S LIBERTY: The Synergistic Transformation of Africa and the West into First-World Partnerships*
6. *A PANDEMIC POETRY, COVID-19*
7. *ALLERGIC TO CORRUPTION: The Legacy of President Michael Sata of Zambia*
8. *BOOK ABOUT SOMETHING: On Ultimate Purpose*
9. *CAMPAIGN FOR AFRICA: A Provocative Crusade for the Economic and Humanitarian Decolonization of Africa*
10. *CHAMPIONS: Application of Common Sense and Biblical Motifs to Succeed in Both Worlds*
11. *CORONAVIRUS PRAYERS*
12. *HH IS THE RIGHT MAN FOR ZAMBIA: And Other Acclaimed Articles on Zambia and Africa*
13. *I BOW: 3500 Prayer Lines of Inspiration & Intercession from the Heart: Volume One*
14. *INTERUNIVERSALISM IN A NUTSHELL: For Iranian Refugee Claimants*
15. *LAW & GRACE: An Expository Study in the Rudiments of Sin and Truth*
16. *LAWS OF INFLUENCE: 7even Lessons in Transformational Leadership*

INDEX

M

maintain their cause, 9
Moses. *See* Prayer of Solomon

P

persisting, 13
Plague of the heart, 7
Prayer of Solomon, vii
professor, 25
promises, 5
protocol, 3

R

regards, 20
revelation, 1
ritual, 8

S

sacrifice. *See* Prayer of
Solomon

Scripts, 6
sin, ix, x, xi, 7, 8
Sinner's Prayer, 8
Struggles of My People, 25, 27
supplication, 11

T

tears, 17
the West, 27
transgressions. *See* Prayer of
Solomon

U

unrighteousness, 8

W

will of God, 10

Z

Zambia, 25, 27, 28, 29